T0338794

credits

Photographer • Annie Noble
Art Direction & Styling • Georgina Brant
Design Layout • Quail Studio
Model • Dayse Lima
Hair and Make Up • Michelle - Court on Camera Creatives

First published in Great Britain in 2021 by
Quail Publishing Limited
Unit 15, Green Farm, Fritwell, Bicester, Oxfordshire,
OX27 7QU
E-mail: info@quailstudio.co.uk

ISBN: 978-1-9162445-6-6

essential
brights

ten hand knit designs
with a pop of colour

quail studio

violet pattern page 28

aqua pattern page 32

pure pattern page 36

essential **brights**

coral pattern page 38

sun pattern page 40

candy pattern page 42

flamingo (short) pattern page 46

flamingo (long) pattern page 46

cobalt pattern page 48

With a joyful pop of colours and fresh whites, Essential Summer Brights by Quail Studio brings a renewed vitality to summer knitting! Using Rowan Kidsilk Haze, Fine Lace, Cotton Glacé, Summerlite DK and Handknit Cotton, knitters will love the textured lace panels and fun colourwork. Featuring relaxed-fit multi-coloured jumpers and cute, cropped tops, this energetic collection oozes positivity and confidence.

cobalt (stripe) pattern page 48

aperol pattern page 50

pina pattern page 52

violet

pattern page 28

aqua

pattern page 32

pure
pattern page 36

coral

pattern page 38

sun

pattern page 40

candy

pattern page 42

flamingo

pattern page 46

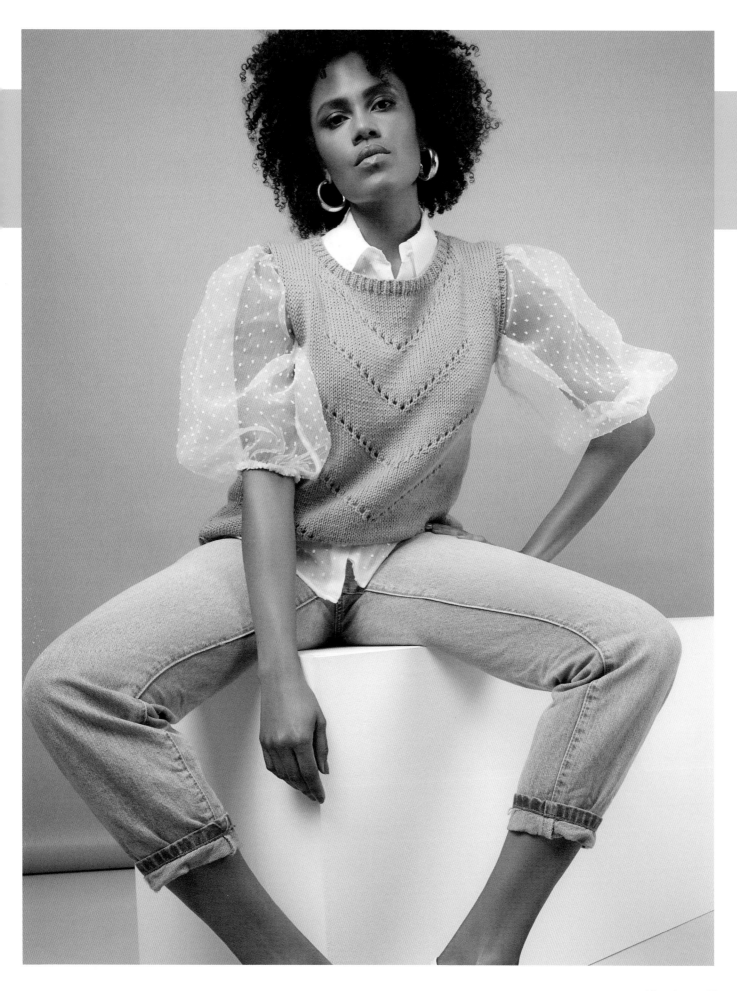

cobalt

pattern page 48

aperol

pattern page 50

pina

pattern page 52

patterns

violet ●●○○

SIZE

To fit bust

81-86	91-97	102-107	112-117	122-127	cm
32-34	36-38	40-42	44-46	48-50	in

Actual bust measurement of garment

92	102	112	122	132	cm
36¼	40¼	44	48	52	in

YARN

Rowan Handknit Cotton

15	15	16	17	18	x 50gm

(photographed in Violet 353)

NEEDLES

1 pair 4½mm (no 7) (US 7) needles
Cable needle

TENSION

28 sts and 30 rows to 10 cm / 4 in measured over
patt using 4½mm (US 7) needles.

SPECIAL ABBREVIATIONS

C3F = slip next 2 sts onto cable needle and leave at
front of work, K1, then K2 from cable needle;
C4F = slip next 2 sts onto cable needle and leave at
front of work, K2, then K2 from cable needle.

BACK

Using 4½mm (US 7) needles cast on 98 [110: 118:
130: 142] sts.
Row 1 (RS): K2, *P2, K2, rep from * to end.
Row 2: P2, *K2, P2, rep from * to end.
These 2 rows form rib.
Cont in rib for a further 5 rows, ending with **WS** facing
for next row.
Row 8 (WS): Rib 4 [7: 2: 5: 8], M1, (rib 3, M1) 30 [32:
38: 40: 42] times, rib 4 [7: 2: 5: 8]. 129 [143: 157:
171: 185] sts.
Now work in patt as folls:
Row 1 (RS): P3, *K4, P3, rep from * to end.
Row 2: K3, *P4, K3, rep from * to end.
Row 3: P3, *C4F, P3, rep from * to end.
Row 4: As row 2.
These 4 rows form patt.
Cont straight until back meas 46 [48: 50: 52: 54] cm,
ending with RS facing for next row.
Shape shoulders and back neck
Next row (RS): * Cast off 8 [10: 12: 13: 15] sts, patt
until there are 32 [37: 41: 47: 51] sts on right needle
and turn, leaving rem sts on a holder.
Work each side of neck separately.
Keeping patt correct, dec 1 st at neck edge of next
5 rows, ending with RS facing for next row, **and at
same time** cast off 9 [10: 12: 14: 15] sts at beg of 2nd
row, then 9 [11: 12: 14: 15] sts at beg of foll alt row.
Cast off rem 9 [11: 12: 14: 16] sts **.
Return to sts left on holder and slip centre 49 [49: 51:
51: 53] sts onto another holder (for neckband). Rejoin
yarn with RS facing and patt to end. Complete
from * to ** to match first side, reversing shapings.

FRONT

Work as given for back until 10 [10: 12: 12: 14] rows
less have been worked than on back to beg of
shoulder shaping, ending with RS facing for next row.
Shape front neck
Next row (RS): Patt 45 [52: 59: 66: 73] sts and turn,
leaving rem sts on a holder.
Work each side of neck separately.
Keeping patt correct, dec 1 st at neck edge of next
8 rows, then on foll 0 [0: 1: 1: 2] alt rows. 37 [44: 50:
57: 63] sts.
Work 1 row, ending with RS facing for next row.
Shape shoulder
Cast off 8 [10: 12: 13: 15] sts at beg of next and foll
0 [1: 2: 0: 2] alt rows, then 9 [11: -: 14: -] sts at beg of
foll 2 [1: -: 2: -] alt rows **and at same time** dec 1 st at
neck edge of next and foll alt row.
Work 1 row.
Cast off rem 9 [11: 12: 14: 16] sts.
Return to sts left on holder and slip centre 39 sts onto
another holder (for neckband). Rejoin yarn with RS
facing and patt to end. Complete to match first side,
reversing shapings.

SLEEVE PATT PANEL (51 [55: 59: 59: 63] sts increasing to 112 [121: 130: 130: 139] sts, and then back down to 88 [95: 102: 102: 109] sts)
Row 1 (RS): K3, (P1, K3) 12 [13: 14: 14: 15] times.
Row 2: P3, (K1, P3) 12 [13: 14: 14: 15] times.
Row 3: C3F, (P1, C3F) 12 [13: 14: 14: 15] times.
Row 4: As row 2.
Rows 5 to 8: As rows 1 to 4.
Rows 9 and 10: As rows 1 and 2.
Row 11: Slip next 2 sts onto cable needle and leave at front of work, inc in next st, then K2 from cable needle, (P1, slip next 2 sts onto cable needle and leave at front of work, inc in next st, then K2 from cable needle) 12 [13: 14: 14: 15] times. 64 [69: 74: 74: 79] sts.
Row 12: P4, (K1, P4) 12 [13: 14: 14: 15] times.
Row 13: K4, (P1, K4) 12 [13: 14: 14: 15] times.
Row 14: As row 12.
Row 15: C4F, (P1, C4F) 12 [13: 14: 14: 15] times.
Rows 16 to 19: As rows 12 to 15.
Row 20: As row 12.
Row 21: K4, (P1, M1P, K4) 12 [13: 14: 14: 15] times. 76 [82: 88: 88: 94] sts.
Row 22: P4, (K2, P4) 12 [13: 14: 14: 15] times.
Row 23: C4F, (P2, C4F) 12 [13: 14: 14: 15] times.
Row 24: As row 22.
Row 25: K4, (P2, K4) 12 [13: 14: 14: 15] times.
Rows 26 to 29: As rows 22 to 25.
Row 30: As row 22.
Row 31: C4F, (P1, M1P, P1, C4F) 12 [13: 14: 14: 15] times. 88 [95: 102: 102: 109] sts.
Row 32: P4, (K3, P4) 12 [13: 14: 14: 15] times.
Row 33: K4, (P3, K4) 12 [13: 14: 14: 15] times.
Row 34: As row 32.
Row 35: C4F, (P3, C4F) 12 [13: 14: 14: 15] times.
Rows 36 to 39: As rows 32 to 35.
Row 40: As row 32.
Row 41: K4, (P1, M1P, P2, K4) 12 [13: 14: 14: 15] times. 100 [108: 116: 116: 124] sts.
Row 42: P4, (K4, P4) 12 [13: 14: 14: 15] times.
Row 43: C4F, (P4, C4F) 12 [13: 14: 14: 15] times.
Row 44: As row 42.
Row 45: K4, (P4, K4) 12 [13: 14: 14: 15] times.
Rows 46 to 49: As rows 42 to 45.
Row 50: As row 42.
Row 51: C4F, (P2, M1P, P2, C4F) 12 [13: 14: 14: 15] times. 112 [121: 130: 130: 139] sts.
Row 52: P4, (K5, P4) 12 [13: 14: 14: 15] times.
Row 53: K4, (P5, K4) 12 [13: 14: 14: 15] times.
Row 54: As row 52.
Row 55: C4F, (P5, C4F) 12 [13: 14: 14: 15] times.
Rows 56 to 91: As rows 52 to 55, 9 times.
Rows 92 to 94: As rows 52 to 54.
Row 95: C4F, (P2, P2tog, P1, C4F) 12 [13: 14: 14: 15] times. 100 [108: 116: 116: 124] sts.
Rows 96 to 107: As rows 42 to 45, 3 times.
Rows 108 to 110: As rows 42 to 44.

Row 111: C4F, (P1, P2tog tbl, P1, C4F) 12 [13: 14: 14: 15] times. 88 [95: 102: 102: 109] sts.
Now rep rows 32 to 35 as required.

SLEEVES
Using 4½mm (US 7) needles cast on 42 [46: 50: 50: 50] sts.
Work in rib as given for back for 7 rows, ending with **WS** facing for next row.
Row 8 (WS): Rib 3 [5: 1: 1: 1], M1, (rib 3 [3: 4: 4: 3], M1) 12 [12: 12: 12: 16] times, rib 3 [5: 1: 1: 1]. 55 [59: 63: 63: 67] sts.
Now work in patt, placing patt panel as folls:
Row 1 (RS): P2, work next 51 [55: 59: 59: 63] sts as row 1 of sleeve patt panel, P2.
Row 2: K2, work next 51 [55: 59: 59: 63] sts as row 2 of sleeve patt panel, K2.
These 2 rows set the sts – centre sts in patt panel with edge sts in rev st st.
Working appropriate rows of patt panel, inc 1 st at each end of 19th [19th: 17th: 9th: 9th] and 4 [4: 5: 7: 7] foll 20th [20th: 18th: 14th: 14th] rows, taking inc sts into rev st st – there will now be 7 [7: 8: 10: 10] sts in rev st st at each side of patt panel.
Cont straight until sleeve meas 44 [44: 45: 45: 45] cm, ending with RS facing for next row.
Cast off in patt.

MAKING UP
Press as described on the information page.
Join right shoulder seam.
Neckband
With RS facing and using 4½mm (US 7) needles, pick up and knit 11 [11: 12: 12: 15] sts down left side of front neck, work across 39 sts on front holder as folls: K2, (K1, K2tog, K1, sl 1, K1, psso, K1) 5 times, K2, pick up and knit 11 [11: 12: 12: 15] sts up right side of front neck, and 5 sts down right side of back neck, work across 49 [49: 51: 51: 53] sts on back holder as folls: K0 [0: 1: 1: 2], (K1, K2tog, K1, sl 1, K1, psso, K1) 7 times, K0 [0: 1: 1: 2], then pick up and knit 5 sts up left side of back neck. 96 [96: 100: 100: 108] sts.
Beg with row 2, work in rib as given for back for 8 rows, ending with **WS** facing for next row.
Cast off in rib (on **WS**).
Join left shoulder and neckband seam. Mark points along side seam edges 20 [21.5: 23: 24.5: 26] cm either side of shoulder seams (to denote base of armhole openings). See information page for finishing instructions, setting in sleeves using the straight cast-off method.

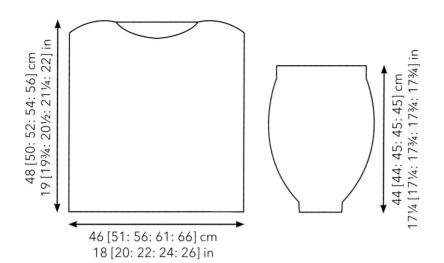

48 [50: 52: 54: 56] cm
19 [19¾: 20½: 21¼: 22] in

46 [51: 56: 61: 66] cm
18 [20: 22: 24: 26] in

44 [44: 45: 45: 45] cm
17¼ [17¼: 17¾: 17¾: 17¾] in

aqua ●●○○

SIZE

To fit bust

81-86	91-97	102-107	112-117	122-127	cm
32-34	36-38	40-42	44-46	48-50	in

Actual bust measurement of garment

88	98.5	108.5	117.5	128	cm
34¾	38¾	42¾	46¼	50½	in

YARN

Rowan Cotton Glace

7	8	8	9	9	x 50gm

(photographed in Aqua 858)

NEEDLES

1 pair 3½mm (no 10/9) (US 4) needles

TENSION

23 sts and 30 rows to 10 cm / 4 in measured over st st using 3½mm (US 4) needles.

FRONT

Using 3½mm (US 4) needles cast on 109 [121: 133: 143: 155] sts.

Beg with a K row, work in st st throughout as folls:
Work 16 rows, ending with RS facing for next row.
Dec 1 st at each end of next and 3 foll 16th rows.
101 [113: 125: 135: 147] sts.
Work 9 [11: 13: 13: 15] rows, ending with RS facing for next row.

Shape armholes

Cast off 5 [6: 7: 7: 8] sts at beg of next 2 rows. 91 [101: 111: 121: 131] sts.
Dec 1 st at each end of next 5 [5: 7: 7: 7] rows, then on foll 4 [6: 6: 7: 8] alt rows. 73 [79: 85: 93: 101] sts.
Work 33 [33: 35: 37: 37] rows, ending with RS facing for next row.

Shape front neck

Next row (RS): K20 [23: 26: 30: 34] and turn, leaving rem sts on a holder.
Work each side of neck separately.
Dec 1 st at neck edge of next 5 [5: 6: 6: 6] rows, then on foll 0 [0: 0: 0: 1] alt row. 15 [18: 20: 24: 27] sts.
Work 0 [0: 1: 1: 1] row, ending with RS facing for next row.

Shape shoulder

Cast off 3 [3: 4: 5: 6] sts at beg of next row, then 3 [4: 4: 5: 6] sts at beg of foll 2 alt rows **and at same time** dec 1 st at neck edge of next and foll 2 alt rows.
Work 1 row.
Cast off rem 3 [4: 5: 6: 6] sts.
Return to sts left on holder, rejoin yarn with RS facing and cast off centre 33 sts, then K to end. Complete to match first side, reversing shapings.

LEFT BACK

Using 3½mm (US 4) needles cast on 18 [24: 31: 38: 47] sts.
Beg with a K row, work in st st throughout as folls:
Work 2 rows, ending with RS facing for next row.
Cast on 8 sts at beg of next row, 7 sts at beg of foll alt row, then 6 sts at beg of foll alt row, 5 sts at beg of foll alt row, then 4 sts at beg of foll alt row, and 3 sts at beg of foll alt row. 51 [57: 64: 71: 80] sts.
Work 1 row, ending with RS facing for next row.
Inc 1 st at beg of next row then at same edge on foll 16 [18: 18: 20: 20] rows, then on foll 7 [7: 8: 7: 7] alt rows, then on 2 [3: 4: 5: 6] foll 4th rows, then on 2 [2: 2: 1: 1] foll 6th rows, then on 1 [0: 0: 0: 0] foll 8th row **and at same time** dec 1 st at end of 3rd and 3 foll 16th rows. 76 [84: 93: 101: 111] sts.
Work 1 [5: 1: 3: 1] rows, ending with RS facing for next row.

Shape armhole

Work 1 row.
Cast off 5 [6: 7: 7: 8] sts at beg of next row. 71 [78: 86: 94: 103] sts.
Dec 1 st at armhole edge of next 5 [5: 7: 7: 7] rows, then on foll 4 [6: 6: 7: 8] alt rows **and at same time** inc

1 st at beg of 5th [next: 5th: next: 3rd] row and 0 [1: 1: 2: 2] foll 8th rows. 63 [69: 75: 83: 91] sts.
Inc 1 st at beg of 2nd [2nd: 4th: 6th: 6th] and foll 10th row, then on foll 12th row. 66 [72: 78: 86: 94] sts.
Work 15 [15: 17: 17: 19] rows, ending with RS facing for next row.

Shape shoulders and back neck
Next row (RS): K9 [12: 14: 19: 21] and turn, leaving rem sts on a holder.
Work each side of neck separately.
Dec 1 st at neck edge of next 4 rows **and at same time** cast off 0 [0: 1: 4: 5] sts at beg of 2nd row, then 2 [4: 4: 5: 6] sts at beg of foll alt row.
Work 1 row.
Cast off rem 3 [4: 5: 6: 6] sts.
Return to sts left on holder, rejoin yarn with RS facing and cast off centre 41 [41: 43: 42: 45] sts, then K to end. 16 [19: 21: 25: 28] sts.
Cast off 3 [3: 4: 5: 6] sts at beg of next row, then 3 [4: 4: 5: 6] sts at beg of foll 2 alt rows **and at same time** dec 1 st at neck edge of next 4 rows.
Work 1 row.
Cast off rem 3 [4: 5: 6: 6] sts.

RIGHT BACK
Using 3½mm (US 4) needles cast on 18 [24: 31: 38: 47] sts.
Beg with a K row, work in st st throughout as folls:
Work 3 rows, ending with **WS** facing for next row.
Cast on 8 sts at beg of next row, 7 sts at beg of foll alt row, then 6 sts at beg of foll alt row, 5 sts at beg of foll alt row, then 4 sts at beg of foll alt row, and 3 sts at beg of foll alt row, ending with RS facing for next row.
51 [57: 64: 71: 80] sts.
Inc 1 st at end of next row then at same edge on foll 16 [18: 18: 20: 20] rows, then on foll 7 [7: 8: 7: 7] alt rows, then on 2 [3: 4: 5: 6] foll 4th rows, then on 2 [2. 2: 1: 1] foll 6th rows, then on 1 [0: 0: 0: 0] foll 8th row **and at same time** dec 1 st at beg of 3rd and 3 foll 16th rows. 76 [84: 93: 101: 111] sts.
Work 1 [5: 1: 3: 1] rows, ending with RS facing for next row.

Shape armhole
Cast off 5 [6: 7: 7: 8] sts at beg of next row. 71 [78: 86: 94: 103] sts.
Work 1 row.
Dec 1 st at armhole edge of next 5 [5: 7: 7: 7] rows, then on foll 4 [6: 6: 7: 8] alt rows **and at same time** inc 1 st at beg of 5th [next: 5th: next: 3rd] row and 0 [1: 1: 2: 2] foll 8th rows. 63 [69: 75: 83: 91] sts.
Inc 1 st at beg of 2nd [2nd: 4th: 6th: 6th] and foll 10th row, then on foll 12th row. 66 [72: 78: 86: 94] sts.
Work 15 [15: 17: 17: 19] rows, ending with RS facing for next row.

Shape shoulders and back neck
Next row (RS): Cast off 3 [3: 4: 5: 6] sts, K until there are 13 [14: 17: 20: 22] sts on right needle and turn, leaving rem sts on a holder.
Work each side of neck separately.
Dec 1 st at neck edge of next 4 rows **and at same time** cast off 3 [4: 4: 5: 6] sts at beg of 2nd row, then 3 [4: 4: 5: 6] sts at beg of foll alt row.
Work 1 row.
Cast off rem 3 [4: 5: 6: 6] sts.
Return to sts left on holder, rejoin yarn with RS facing and cast off centre 41 [41: 43: 43: 45] sts, then K to end. 9 [14: 14: 18: 21] sts.
Dec 1 st at neck edge of next 4 rows **and at same time** cast off 0 [2: 0: 3: 5] sts at beg of 3rd row. 5 [8: 10: 11: 12] sts.
Cast off 2 [4: 5: 5: 6] sts at beg of next row.
Work 1 row.
Cast off rem 3 [4: 5: 6: 6] sts.

MAKING UP
Press as described on the information page.
Join both side seams.
Hem and back edging
Using 3½mm (US 4) needles cast on 5 sts.
Row 1 (RS): K3, (yfwd) twice, K2. 7 sts.
Row 2: K2, (K1, P1) into double yfwd of previous row, K3.
Rows 3 and 4: Knit.
Row 5: K3, (yfwd) twice, K2tog, (yfwd) twice, K2. 10 sts.
Row 6: K2, (K1, P1) into double yfwd of previous row, K1, (K1, P1) into double yfwd of previous row, K3.
Row 7: Knit.
Row 8: Cast off 5 sts, K to end. 5 sts.
These 8 rows form patt.
Cont in patt until straight edge of edging, when slightly stretched and beg and ending at shoulder edges, fits neatly down left back shaped opening edge, across front cast-on edge and then up shaped right back opening edge, sewing in place as you go along, easing edging around curved edges, ending after patt row 8 and with RS facing for next row.
Cast off.
Lay left back over right back, matching neck and shoulder edges, and neatly sew edges together. Join shoulder seams.
Neck edging
Beg and ending at one shoulder seam, work as given for hem and back edging, making and attaching a strip that neatly fits around entire neck edge.
Join cast-on and cast-off ends.
Armhole edgings (both alike)
Beg and ending at top of side seam, work as given for hem and back edging, making and attaching a strip that neatly fits around armhole edge.
Join cast-on and cast-off ends.
See information page for finishing instructions.

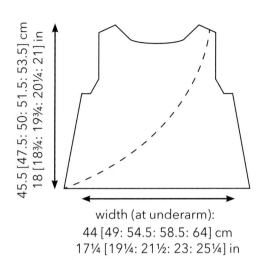

45.5 [47.5: 50: 51.5: 53.5] cm
18 [18¾: 19¾: 20¼: 21] in

width (at underarm):
44 [49: 54.5: 58.5: 64] cm
17¼ [19¼: 21½: 23: 25¼] in

47 [52.5: 57.5: 62: 67] cm
18½ [20½: 22½: 24½: 26¼] in

pure ●○○○

SIZE

To fit bust

81-86	91-97	102-107	112-117	122-127	cm
32-34	36-38	40-42	44-46	48-50	in

Actual bust measurement of garment

100	111	121	131	141	cm
39¼	43¾	47¾	51½	55½	in

YARN

Rowan Summerlite DK

5	6	6	7	7	x 50gm

(photographed in White 465)

NEEDLES

3¼mm (no 10) (US 3) needles
3¾mm (no 9) (US 5) needles

TENSION

22sts and 30 rows to 10cm/ 4in measured over st st using 3¾mm needles.

BACK

Using 3¼mm needles cast on 111 [121: 133: 145: 155] sts.
Row 1 (RS): *K1, P1 rep from * to last st, K1.
Row 2: P1, *K1, P1, rep from * to end.
Last 2 rows set rib, work in rib until work meas 8cm, ending with a WS row, dec 1 st in middle of last row. 110 [120: 132: 144: 154] sts.
Change to 3¾mm needles
Starting with a K row, work in st st until work meas 25 [26: 27: 28: 29] cm, ending with a WS row.
Shape armholes
Cast off 5 sts at beg of next 2 rows. 100 [110: 122: 134: 144] sts.
Next Row (RS): K2, Sl 1, K1, psso, K to last 4 sts, K2tog, K2. 98 [108: 120: 132: 142] sts.
Next Row: Purl.
Rep last 2 rows once more. 96 [106: 118: 130: 140] sts **
Cont in st st until armhole meas 19 [20: 21: 22: 23] cm, ending with a WS row.
Shape shoulders and back neck
Cast off 15 [17: 20: 22: 24] sts at beg of next 4 rows. 36 [38: 38: 42: 44] sts.
Leave rem sts on a stitch holder.

FRONT

Work as for back to **
Cont in st st until 22 rows less have been worked than start of shoulder shaping, ending with a WS row.
Shape neck
Next Row (RS): K37 [42: 46: 50: 55] sts and turn, leaving rem sts on a stitch holder.
Dec 1 st at neck edge on foll 3rd row to 30 [34: 40: 44: 48] sts.
Work 1 row.
Next Row (RS): Cast off 15 [17: 20: 22: 24] sts at beg of next and foll alt row.
Fasten off.
With RS facing, slip next 22 [22: 26: 30: 30] sts onto a stitch holder for front neck, rejoin yarn and work as for other side of neck, reversing shapings.

MAKING UP

Press as described on the information page.
Join right shoulder seam using mattress stitch.
Neckband
With RS facing and using 3¼ mm (US 3) needles pick up and knit 20 sts on right front neck, knit 22 [22: 26: 30: 30] sts from front neck st holder, pick up and knit 20 sts up left front neck, knit 36 [38: 38: 42: 44] sts from back neck st holder. 98 [100: 104: 112: 114] sts.
Next Row (WS): K1, P1 to end.
Rep last row until neckband meas 3cm, ending with a WS row.

Cast off in rib with larger needle.

Join left shoulder and neckband seams using mattress stitch.

Armhole edging

With RS facing and using 3¼mm (US 3) needles pick up and knit 5 sts from cast off for underarm, pick up and knit 42 [44: 46: 48: 50] sts up to shoulder seam, pick up and knit 42 [44: 46: 48: 50] sts down to underarm cast off, pick up and knit 5 sts from cast off. 94 [98: 102: 106: 110] sts.

Next Row (WS): K1, P1 to end.

Rep last row until armhole edging meas 3cm, ending with a WS row.

Cast off in rib.

Work other side to match.

Join side and armhole edge seams using mattress stitch, leaving lower 8cm of side seam open.

See information page for finishing instructions.

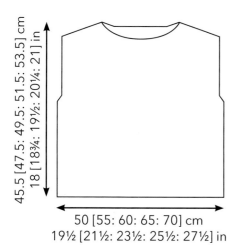

45.5 [47.5: 49.5: 51.5: 53.5] cm
18 [18¾: 19½: 20¼: 21] in

50 [55: 60: 65: 70] cm
19½ [21½: 23½: 25½: 27½] in

coral ●○○○

SIZE

To fit bust

81-86	91-97	102-107	112-117	122-127	cm
32-34	36-38	40-42	44-46	48-50	in

Actual bust measurement of garment

97	107	117	127	137	cm
38¼	42¼	46	50	54	in

YARN

Rowan Summerlite DK and Kidsilk Haze
A DK - Cantaloupe 456

5	5	6	6	7	x50gm

B KSH - Golden Poppy 683

3	3	3	3	4	x 25gm

NEEDLES

1 pair 4½mm (no 7) (US 7) needles
4½mm (no 7) (US 7) circular needle no more than 30 cm long

TENSION

20 sts and 27 rows to 10 cm / 4 in measured over st st using 4½mm (US 7) needles and one strand each of yarns A and B held together.

BACK

Using 4½mm (US 7) needles and one strand each of yarns A and B held together cast on 100 [110: 120: 130: 140] sts.
Row 1 (RS): K4, *P2, K3, rep from * to last st, K1.
Row 2: K1, P3, *K2, P3, rep from * to last st, K1.
These 2 rows form rib.
Cont in rib until work meas 10 cm, ending with RS facing for next row.
Place markers at both ends of last row.
Next row (RS): K16 [17: 19: 21: 22], K2tog, (K31 [35: 38: 41: 45], K2tog) twice, K16 [17: 19: 21: 22]. 97 [107: 117: 127: 137] sts.
Beg with a **purl** row, cont in st st throughout as folls:
Work 123 [129: 133: 139: 145] rows, ending with RS facing for next row. (Back should meas approx 56 [58: 60: 62: 64] cm.)
Shape shoulders and back neck
Next row (RS): Cast off 14 [16: 18: 21: 23] sts, K until there are 18 [21: 23: 25: 27] sts on right needle and turn, leaving rem sts on a holder.
Work each side of neck separately.
Cast off 4 sts at beg of next row.
Cast off rem 14 [17: 19: 21: 23] sts.
Return to sts left on holder and slip centre 33 [33: 35: 35: 37] sts onto another holder (for neckband). Rejoin yarn with RS facing and K to end. Complete to match first side, reversing shapings.

FRONT

Using 4½mm (US 7) needles and one strand each of yarns A and B held together cast on 100 [110: 120: 130: 140] sts.
Beg with row 1, work in rib as given for back for 5 cm, ending with RS facing for next row.
Place markers at both ends of last row.
Next row (RS): K16 [17: 19: 21: 22], K2tog, (K31 [35: 38: 41: 45], K2tog) twice, K16 [17: 19: 21: 22]. 97 [107: 117: 127: 137] sts.
Beg with a **purl** row, cont in st st throughout as folls:
Work 85 [91: 93: 99: 101] rows, ending with RS facing for next row.
Divide for front neck
Next row (RS): K48 [53: 58: 63: 68] and turn, leaving rem sts on a holder.
Work each side of neck separately.
Dec 1 st at neck edge of next 4 [4: 4: 4: 2] rows, then on foll 16 [16: 17: 17: 20] alt rows. 28 [33: 37: 42: 46] sts.
Work 1 row, ending with RS facing for next row.
Shape shoulder
Cast off 14 [16: 18: 21: 23] sts at beg of next row.
Work 1 row.
Cast off rem 14 [17: 19: 21: 23] sts.
Return to sts left on holder and slip centre st onto another holder (for neckband). Rejoin yarn with RS facing and K to end. 48 [53: 58: 63: 68] sts. Complete to match first side, reversing shapings.

MAKING UP

Press as described on the information page.
Join both shoulder seams using back stitch, or mattress stitch if preferred.

Neckband

With RS facing and using 4½mm (US 7) circular needle, pick up and knit 36 [36: 41: 41: 46] sts down left side of front neck, K st on front holder and mark this st with a coloured thread, pick up and knit 36 [36: 41: 41: 46] sts up right side of front neck, and 4 sts down right side of back neck, 33 [33: 35: 35: 37] sts on back holder inc 1 [1: 4: 4: 2] sts evenly, then pick up and knit 4 sts up left side of back neck. 115 [115: 130: 130: 140] sts.

Round 1 (RS): *K3, P2, rep from * to end.
This round forms rib.
Keeping rib correct, cont as folls:

Round 2: Rib to within 1 st of marked st, slip next 2 sts as though to K2tog (marked st is second of these 2 sts), K1, then pass 2 slipped sts over, rib to end. 113 [113: 128: 128: 138] sts.

Round 3: Rib to marked st, K marked st, rib to end.
Rep last 2 rounds 5 times more. 103 [103: 118: 118: 128] sts.
Cast off in rib, still dec either side of marked st as before.

Mark points along side seam edges 20 [21.5: 23: 24.5: 26] cm either side of shoulder seams (to denote base of armhole openings). Join side seams below these markers, leaving seams open below lower markers – front is 5 cm shorter than back.

Armhole borders (both alike)

With RS facing and using 4½mm (US 7) circular needle, pick up and knit 81 [86: 91: 101: 106] sts evenly all round armhole edge.

Round 1 (RS): K2, *P2, K3, rep from * to last 4 sts, P2, K2.
This round forms rib.
Keeping rib correct, cont as folls:

Round 2: K1, sl 1, K1, psso, rib to last 3 sts, K2tog, K1. 79 [84: 89: 99: 104] sts.

Round 3: K2, rib to last 2 sts, K2.
Rep last 2 rounds twice more. 75 [80: 85: 95: 100] sts.
Cast off in rib, still dec as before.
See information page for finishing instructions.

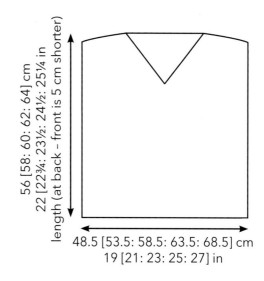

56 [58: 60: 62: 64] cm
22 [22¾: 23½: 24½: 25¼] in
length (at back – front is 5 cm shorter)

48.5 [53.5: 58.5: 63.5: 68.5] cm
19 [21: 23: 25: 27] in

sun ●●○○

SIZE

To fit bust

81-86	91-97	102-107	112-117	122-127	cm
32-34	36-38	40-42	44-46	48-50	in

Actual bust measurement of garment

101.5	110	121.5	130	141.5	cm
40	43¼	47¾	51¼	55¾	in

YARN

Rowan Summerlite DK and Kidsilk Haze

A DK – Summer 453

6	7	7	8	8	x 50gm

B KSH - Eve Green 684

4	4	5	5	6	x 25gm

NEEDLES

1 pair 5mm (no 6) (US 8) needles

TENSION

14 sts and 28 rows to 10 cm / 4 in measured over patt using 5mm (US 8) needles and one strand each of yarns A and B held together.

BACK

Using 5mm (US 8) needles and one strand each of yarns A and B held together cast on 71 [77: 86: 92: 98] sts.

Row 1 (RS): K2, *P1, K2, rep from * to end.
Row 2: P2, *K1, P2, rep from * to end.
These 2 rows form rib.
Cont in rib for a further 10 rows, - [-: dec: dec: inc] - [-: 1: 1: 1] st at end of last row and ending with RS facing for next row. 71 [77: 85: 91: 99] sts.
Now work in patt as folls:
Rows 1 and 2: Purl.
Row 3 (RS): K1, *yfwd, sl 1, K1, psso, rep from * to end.
Rows 4 to 6: Purl.
Row 7: *K2tog, yfwd, rep from * to last st, K1.
Row 8: Purl.
These 8 rows form patt.
Cont straight until back meas 55 [57: 59: 61: 63] cm, ending with RS facing for next row.
Shape shoulders and back neck
Next row (RS): * Cast off 7 [8: 9: 10: 11] sts, patt until there are 18 [20: 22: 24: 26] sts on right needle and turn, leaving rem sts on a holder.
Work each side of neck separately.
Dec 1 st at neck edge of next 3 rows, ending with RS facing for next row, **and at same time** cast off 7 [8: 9: 10: 11] sts at beg of 2nd row.
Cast off rem 8 [9: 10: 11: 12] sts **.
Return to sts left on holder and slip centre 21 [21: 23: 23: 25] sts onto another holder (for neckband).
Rejoin yarn with RS facing and patt to end. Complete from * to ** to match first side, reversing shapings.

FRONT

Work as given for back until 12 [12: 14: 14: 16] rows less have been worked than on back to beg of shoulder shaping, ending with RS facing for next row.
Shape front neck
Next row (RS): Patt 29 [32: 36: 39: 43] sts and turn, leaving rem sts on a holder.
Work each side of neck separately.
Keeping patt correct, dec 1 st at neck edge of next 4 rows, then on foll 3 [3: 4: 4: 5] alt rows. 22 [25: 28: 31: 34] sts.
Work 1 row, ending with RS facing for next row.
Shape shoulder
Cast off 7 [8: 9: 10: 11] sts at beg of next and foll alt row.
Work 1 row.
Cast off rem 8 [9: 10: 11: 12] sts.
Return to sts left on holder and slip centre 13 sts onto another holder (for neckband). Rejoin yarns with RS facing and patt to end. Complete to match first side, reversing shapings.

SLEEVES

Using 5mm (US 8) needles and one strand each of yarns A and B held together cast on 32 [32: 32: 32: 35] sts.

Work in rib as given for back for 14 rows, dec [inc: inc: inc: -] 1 [1: 1: 1: -] st at end of last row and ending with RS facing for next row. 31 [33: 33: 33: 35] sts.

Now work in patt as folls:

Rows 1 and 2: Purl.

Row 3 (RS): K1, *yfwd, sl 1, K1, psso, rep from * to end.

Rows 4 to 6: Purl, inc 0 [0: 0: 1: 1] st at each end of row 5. 31 [33: 35: 35: 37] sts.

Row 7: (Inc in first st) 0 [1: 1: 0: 0] time, K0 [1: 1: 1: 1], *K2tog, yfwd, rep from * to last 1 [3: 3: 2: 2] sts, K1 [2: 2: 2: 2], (inc in last st) 0 [1: 1: 0: 0] time. 31 [35: 37: 35: 37] sts.

Row 8: Purl.

These 8 rows form patt and beg sleeve shaping.

Cont in patt, shaping sides by inc 1 st at each end of next [7th: 7th: 3rd: 3rd] and every foll 10th [8th: 8th: 6th: 6th] row to 47 [39: 57: 47: 57] sts, then on every foll 12th [10th: 10th: 8th: 8th] row until there are 51 [55: 59: 63: 67] sts, taking inc sts into patt.

Cont straight until sleeve meas 46 [46: 47: 47: 47] cm, ending with RS facing for next row.

Cast off in patt.

MAKING UP

Press as described on the information page.

Join right shoulder seam using mattress stitch or back stitch if preferred.

Neckband

With RS facing, using 5mm (US 8) needles and one strand each of yarns A and B held together, pick up and knit 12 [12: 14: 14: 16] sts down left side of front neck, K across 13 sts on front holder, pick up and knit 12 [12: 14: 14: 16] sts up right side of front neck, and 3 sts down right side of back neck, K across 21 [21: 23: 23: 25] sts on back holder inc 1 st at centre, then pick up and knit 3 sts up left side of back neck. 65 [65: 71: 71: 77] sts.

Beg with row 2, work in rib as given for back for 8 rows, ending with **WS** facing for next row.

Cast off in rib (on **WS**).

Join left shoulder and neckband seam. Mark points along side seam edges 19 [20.5: 22: 23.5: 25] cm either side of shoulder seams (to denote base of armhole openings). See information page for finishing instructions, setting in sleeves using the straight cast-off method.

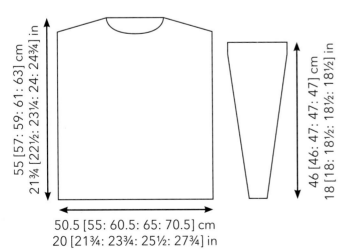

55 [57: 59: 61: 63] cm
21¾ [22½: 23¼: 24: 24¾] in

46 [46: 47: 47: 47] cm
18 [18: 18½: 18½: 18½] in

50.5 [55: 60.5: 65: 70.5] cm
20 [21¾: 23¾: 25½: 27¾] in

candy ●○○○

SIZE
To fit bust

81-86	91-97	102-107	112-117	122-127	cm
32-34	36-38	40-42	44-46	48-50	in

Actual bust measurement of garment

112	123	133	143	153	cm
44	48½	52¼	56¼	60¼	in

YARN
Rowan Kidsilk Haze and Fine Lace

A (KSH) Candy Girl 606						
2	2	3	3	4	x 25gm
B (FL) Ruby 953						
1	1	2	2	2	x 50gm
C (KSH) Blushes 583						
2	2	3	3	4	x 25gm
D (FL) Azalea 956						
1	1	2	2	2	x 50gm
E (KSH) Crown Jewel 690						
2	2	3	3	4	x 25gm
F (FL) Antique 921						
1	1	2	2	2	x 50gm
G (KSH) Aura 676						
3	3	3	4	4	x 25gm
H (FL) Pidgeon 950						
2	2	2	2	2	x 50gm

NEEDLES
4½mm (no 7) (US 7) needles
6½mm (no 3) (US 10.5) needles

TENSION
24 sts and 26 rows to 10 cm / 4 in, over K1, P1 rib using 4½mm (US 7) needles holding 2 strands of kidsilk haze and 1 of fine lace together 14 sts and 20 rows to 10 cm / 4 in, over st st, using 6½mm (US 10.5) needles holding 2 strands of kidsilk haze and 1 of fine lace together

Pattern note – when working on the front pieces add new yarn on the side seams when needed.

BACK
Using 4½mm (US 7) needles and holding 2 strands of yarn A and 1 of B together cast on 136 [148: 160: 172: 184] sts.
Row 1 (RS): (K1, P1) to end.
Repeat last row until work meas 6cm, ending with a WS row.
Next Row (WS): * P1, P2tog, rep from * to last stitch, P1. 91 [99: 107: 115: 123] sts.
Change to 6½mm (US 10.5) needles
Next Row (RS): Knit
Next Row (WS): * P5, P2tog, rep from * to last 0 [8: 16: 10: 4] sts, P 0 [8: 16: 10: 4] sts. 78 [86: 94: 100: 106] sts.
Starting with a K row, work in st st until work meas 10 [11, 12, 13, 14] cm from cast on edge, ending with a WS row.
Change to 2 strands of yarn C and 1 of D until work meas 20 [21: 22: 23: 24] cm from cast on edge, ending with a WS row.
Change to 2 strands of yarn E and 1 of F until work meas 30 [31: 32: 33: 34] cm from cast on edge, ending with a WS row.
Change to 2 strands of yarn G and 1 of H until work meas 59 [60: 61: 62: 63] cm from cast on edge, ending with a WS row.
Shape shoulders and back neck
Cast off 14 [16: 17: 18: 19] sts at beg of foll 4 rows.
22 [22: 26: 28: 30] sts.
Cast off rem sts.

LEFT FRONT
Pattern note: Slip the first stitch of every WS row.

Using 4½mm (US 7) needles and holding 2 strands of yarn A and 1 of B together cast on 68 [74: 80: 86: 92] sts.
Row 1 (RS): (K1, P1) to end.
Rep last row until work meas 6cm, ending with a WS row.
Next Row (WS): (P1, K1) twice, P1, *P1, P2tog rep from * to end. 47 [51: 55: 59: 63] sts.
Change to 6½mm (US 10.5) needles
Row 1 (RS): K to last 6 sts, (P1, K1) three times.
Row 2: (P1, K1) three times, P to end.
Keeping pattern correct with 6 sts on rib, repeat last 2 rows until work meas 10 [11: 12: 13: 14] cm from cast on edge, ending with a WS row.

Change to 2 strands of yarn C and 1 of D until work meas 20 [21: 22: 23: 24] cm from cast on edge, ending with a WS row.
Change to 2 strands of yarn E and 1 of F until work meas 30 [31: 32: 33: 34] cm from cast on edge, ending with a WS row.
Change to 2 strands of yarn G and 1 of H.
Shape front neck
Next Row (RS): K to last 9 sts, Sl 1, K1, psso, K1, (P1, K1) three times. 46 [50: 54: 58: 62] sts.
Working decreases as set above, dec 1 st on every foll 4th row to 33 [37: 39: 41: 43] sts.
Continue without shaping until front matches length of back to start of shoulder shaping, ending with a WS row.
Shape shoulders
Keeping rib pattern correct cast off 14 [16: 17: 18: 19] sts at beg of next and foll alt row. 5 sts. Leave rem sts on a stitch holder, **do not break off yarn**.

RIGHT FRONT
Pattern note: Slip the first stitch of every RS row.

Using 4½mm (US 7) needles and holding 2 strands of yarn A and 1 of B together cast on 68 [74: 80: 86: 92] sts.
Row 1 (RS): (K1, P1) to end.
Rep last row until work meas 6cm, ending with a WS row.
Next Row (WS): * P1, P2tog rep from * to last 5sts, P1, (K1, P1) twice. 47 [51: 55: 59: 63] sts.
Change to 6½mm (US 10.5) needles
Row 1 (RS): (K1, P1) three times, K to end.
Row 2: P to last 6sts, (K1, P1) three times.
Keeping pattern correct with 6 sts on rib, repeat last 2 rows until work meas 10 [11: 12: 13: 14] cm from cast on edge, ending with a WS row.
Change to 2 strands of yarn C and 1 of D until work meas 20 [21: 22: 23: 24] cm from cast on edge, ending with a WS row.
Change to 2 strands of yarn E and 1 of F until work meas 30 [31: 32: 33: 34] cm from cast on edge, ending with a WS row.
Change to 2 strands of yarn G and 1 of H.
Shape front neck
Next Row (RS): (K1, P1) three times, K1, K2tog, K to end. 46 [50: 54: 58: 62] sts.
Working decreases as set above, dec 1 st on every foll 4th row to 33 [37: 39: 41: 43] sts.
Continue without shaping until front matches length of back to start of shoulder shaping, ending with a RS row.

Shape shoulders
Keeping rib pattern correct cast off 14 [16: 17: 18: 19] sts at beg of next and foll alt row. 5 sts. Leave rem sts on a stitch holder, **do not break off yarn.**

SLEEVES
Using 4½mm (US 7) needles and holding 2 strands of yarn A and 1 of B together cast on 48 [50: 52: 56: 58] sts.
Row 1 (RS): K1, P1 to end.
Rep last row until work meas 6cm, ending with a WS row.
Next Row (WS): Inc 8 [8: 10: 8: 8] sts evenly across the row. 56 [58: 62: 64: 66] sts.
Change to 6½mm (US 10.5) needles
Change to 2 strands of yarn G and 1 of H, starting with a K row work in st st until work meas 16 [17: 18: 19: 20] cm from cast on edge, ending with a WS row.
Change to 2 strands of yarn A and 1 of B until work meas 22.5 [23.5: 24: 25.5: 26.5] cm from cast on edge, ending with a WS row.
Change to 2 strands of yarn C and 1 of D until work meas 29 [30: 31: 32: 33: 34] cm from cast on edge, ending with a WS row.
Change to 2 strands of yarn E and 1 of F until work meas 35.5 [36.5: 37.5: 38.5: 39.5] cm from cast on edge, ending with a WS row.
Change to 2 strands of yarn G and 1 of H until work meas 46 [47: 48: 49: 50] cm from cast on edge, ending with a WS row.
Cast off.

MAKING UP
Press as described on the information page.
Join both shoulder seams using mattress stitch.
Neckband
Slip 5 sts from holder for left front panel onto 6.5mm (US 10.5) needles, work in rib until work reaches half way to back of neck.
Cast off.
Work other side to match.
Join cast off edges together and join to back neck.
Placing a pin on front and back 20 [21: 22: 23: 24] cm down from shoulder seam, sew sleeves in place.
Join sleeve seams and then side seams using mattress stitch.
See information for finishing instructions.

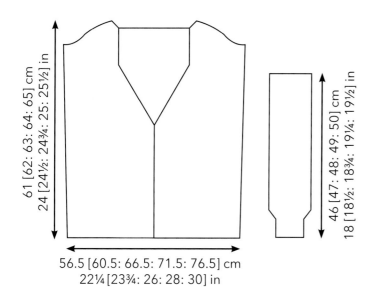

61 [62: 63: 64: 65] cm
24 [24½: 24¾: 25: 25½] in

46 [47: 48: 49: 50] cm
18 [18½: 18¾: 19¼: 19½] in

56.5 [60.5: 66.5: 71.5: 76.5] cm
22¼ [23¾: 26: 28: 30] in

flamingo ●●○○

SIZE
To fit bust

| 81-86 | 91-97 | 102-107 | 112-117 | 122-127 | cm |
| 32-34 | 36-38 | 40-42 | 44-46 | 48-50 | in |

Actual bust measurement of garment

| 91 | 101 | 111 | 121 | 131 | cm |
| 35¾ | 39¾ | 43¾ | 47¾ | 51½ | in |

YARN
Rowan Handknit Cotton
Shorter Version

| 6 | 6 | 7 | 7 | 8 | x 50gm |

(photographed in Flamingo 368)
Longer Version

| 6 | 7 | 7 | 8 | 8 | x 50gm |

(photographed in Gooseberry 219)

NEEDLES
1 pair 4mm (no 8) (US 6) needles
1 pair 4½mm (no 7) (US 7) needles

TENSION
20 sts and 28 rows to 10 cm / 4 in measured over st st using 4½mm (US 7) needles.

BACK
Using 4mm (US 6) needles cast on 91 [101: 111: 121: 131] sts.
Row 1 (RS): K1, *P1, K1, rep from * to end.
Row 2: P1, *K1, P1, rep from * to end.
These 2 rows form rib.
Work in rib for a further 2 rows, ending with RS facing for next row.
Change to 4½mm (US 7) needles.
Shorter Version;
Beg with a K row, work in st st until back meas 28 [28.5: 29: 29.5: 30] cm, ending with RS facing for next row.
Longer Version;
Beg with a K row, work in st st until back meas 36 [36.5: 37: 37.5: 38] cm, ending with RS facing for next row.

Shape armholes
Cast off 3 [4: 5: 6: 7] sts at beg of next 2 rows. 85 [93: 101: 109: 117] sts.
Dec 1 st at each end of next 3 [5: 5: 5: 5] rows, then on foll 3 [3: 4: 5: 5] alt rows. 73 [77: 83: 89: 97] sts.
Cont straight until armhole meas 19 [20.5: 22: 23.5: 25] cm, ending with RS facing for next row.
Shape back neck and shoulders
Next row (RS): * Cast off 5 [6: 6: 7: 8] sts, K until there are 13 [14: 16: 18: 20] sts on right needle and turn, leaving rem sts on a holder.
Work each side of neck separately.
Dec 1 st at neck edge of next 3 rows, ending with RS facing for next row, **and at same time** cast off 5 [6: 6: 7: 8] sts at beg of 2nd row.
Cast off rem 5 [5: 7: 8: 9] sts **.
Return to sts left on holder and slip centre 37 [37: 39: 39: 41] sts onto another holder (for neckband). Rejoin yarn with RS facing and K to end. Complete to match first side from * to **, reversing shapings.

FRONT
Using 4mm (US 6) needles cast on 91 [101: 111: 121: 131] sts.
Work in rib as given back for 4 rows, ending with RS facing for next row.
Change to 4½mm (US 7) needles.
Work in patt as folls:
Row 1 (RS): K44 [49: 54: 59: 64], K2tog, yfwd, K45 [50: 55: 60: 65].
Row 2 and every foll alt row: Purl.
Row 3: K42 [47: 52: 57: 62], K2tog, yfwd, K3, yfwd, sl 1, K1, psso, K42 [47: 52: 57: 62].
Row 5: K40 [45: 50: 55: 60], K2tog, yfwd, K7, yfwd, sl 1, K1, psso, K40 [45: 50: 55: 60].
Row 7: K38 [43: 48: 53: 58], K2tog, yfwd, K11, yfwd, sl 1, K1, psso, K38 [43: 48: 53: 58].
Row 9: K36 [41: 46: 51: 56], K2tog, yfwd, K15, yfwd, sl 1, K1, psso, K36 [41: 46: 51: 56].
Row 11: K34 [39: 44: 49: 54], K2tog, yfwd, K19, yfwd, sl 1, K1, psso, K34 [39: 44: 49: 54].

Row 13: K32 [37: 42: 47: 52], K2tog, yfwd, K23, yfwd, sl 1, K1, psso, K32 [37: 42: 47: 52].
Row 15: K30 [35: 40: 45: 50], K2tog, yfwd, K27, yfwd, sl 1, K1, psso, K30 [35: 40: 45: 50].
Row 17: K28 [33: 38: 43: 48], K2tog, yfwd, K31, yfwd, sl 1, K1, psso, K28 [33: 38: 43: 48].
Row 19: K26 [31: 36: 41: 46], K2tog, yfwd, K35, yfwd, sl 1, K1, psso, K26 [31: 36: 41: 46].
Row 21: K24 [29: 34: 39: 44], K2tog, yfwd, K39, yfwd, sl 1, K1, psso, K24 [29: 34: 39: 44].
Row 22: Purl.
These 22 rows form patt.

Shorter Version;
Repeat these 22 rows until front meas 28 [28.5: 29: 29.5: 30] cm, ending with RS facing for next row.
Longer Version;
Repeat these 22 rows until front meas 36 [36.5: 37: 37.5: 38] cm, ending with RS facing for next row.

Shape armholes
Keeping patt correct, cast off 3 [4: 5: 6: 7] sts at beg of next 2 rows. 85 [93: 101: 109: 117] sts.
Dec 1 st at each end of next 3 [5: 5: 5: 5] rows, then on foll 3 [3: 4: 5: 5] alt rows. 73 [77: 83: 89: 97] sts.
Cont straight until 12 [12: 14: 14: 16] rows less have been worked than on back to beg of shoulder shaping, ending with RS facing for next row.
Shape front neck
Next row (RS): Patt 23 [25: 28: 31: 35] sts and turn, leaving rem sts on a holder.
Work each side of neck separately.
Keeping patt correct, dec 1 st at neck edge of next 6 rows, then on foll 2 [2: 3: 3: 4] alt rows. 15 [17: 19: 22: 25] sts.
Work 1 row.
Shape shoulder
Cast off 5 [6: 6: 7: 8] sts at beg of next and foll alt row.
Work 1 row.
Cast off rem 5 [5: 7: 8: 9] sts.
Return to sts left on holder and slip centre 27 sts onto another holder (for neckband). Rejoin yarn with RS facing and patt to end. Complete to match first side, reversing shapings.

MAKING UP
Press as described on the information page.
Join right shoulder seam using back stitch, or mattress stitch if preferred.
Neckband
With RS facing and using 4mm (US 6) needles, pick up and knit 12 [12: 14: 14: 16] sts down left side of front neck, K across 27 sts on front holder, pick up and knit 12 [12: 14: 14: 16] sts up right side of front neck, and 3 sts down right side of back neck, K across 37 [37: 39: 39: 41] sts on back holder inc 1 st at centre, then pick up and knit 3 sts up left side of back neck. 95 [95: 101: 101: 107] sts.

Beg with row 2, work in rib as given for back for 4 rows, ending with **WS** facing for next row.
Cast off in rib (on **WS**).
Join left shoulder and neckband seam.
Armhole borders (both alike)
With RS facing and using 4mm (US 6) needles, pick up and knit 82 [90: 98: 106: 114] sts evenly all round armhole edge.
Beg with row 2, work in rib as given for back for 2 rows, ending with **WS** facing for next row.
Cast off in rib (on **WS**).
See information page for finishing instructions.

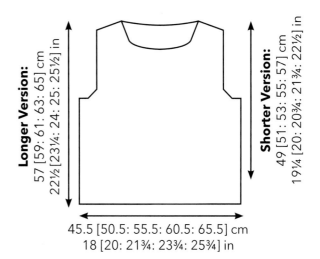

Longer Version: 57 [59: 61: 63: 65] cm 22½ [23¾: 24: 25: 25½] in
Shorter Version: 49 [51: 53: 55: 57] cm 19¼ [20: 20¾: 21¾: 22½] in

45.5 [50.5: 55.5: 60.5: 65.5] cm
18 [20: 21¾: 23¾: 25¾] in

cobalt ●○○○

SIZE
To fit bust

81-86	91-97	102-107	112-117	122-127	cm
32-34	36-38	40-42	44-46	48-50	in

Actual bust measurement of garment

113	121.5	133	141.5	153	cm
44½	47¾	52¼	55¾	60¼	in

YARN
Single colour
Rowan Kidsilk Haze

6	7	7	8	8	x 25gm

(photographed in Laguna 685)
Striped colour
Rowan Kidsilk Haze
A Candy Girl 606

3	3	3	3	4	x 25gm

B Eve Green 684

2	2	2	2	2	x 25gm

C Peacock 671

2	3	3	3	3	x 25gm

NEEDLES
1 pair 6mm (no 4) (US 10) needles
1 pair 6½mm (no 3) (US 10½) needles

TENSION
14 sts and 18 rows to 10 cm / 4 in measured over
st st using 6½mm (US 10.5) needles and yarn held
DOUBLE.

BACK
Using 6mm (US 10) needles and yarn DOUBLE, cast
on 79 [85: 93: 99: 107] sts **loosely.** Refer to the stripe
sequence below if making the striped colour version.

Row 1 (RS): K1, *P1, K1, rep from * to end.
Row 2: P1, *K1, P1, rep from * to end.
These 2 rows form rib.
Cont in rib for a further 4 rows, ending with RS facing
for next row.
Change to 6½mm (US 10.5) needles.
Beg with a K row, now work in st st until back meas
36 [36.5: 37: 37.5: 38] cm, ending with RS facing for
next row.
Shape armholes
Cast off 3 sts at beg of next 2 rows. 73 [79: 87:
93: 101] sts.
Dec 1 st at each end of next 3 [3: 5: 5: 7] rows, then on
foll 1 [2: 2: 3: 3] alt rows. 65 [69: 73: 77: 81] sts.
Cont straight until armhole meas 21 [22.5: 24:
25.5: 26] cm, ending with RS facing for next row.
Shape shoulders and back neck
Next row (RS): * Cast off 5 [6: 6: 7: 7] sts, K until there
are 13 [14: 15: 16: 18] sts on right needle and turn,
leaving rem sts on a holder.
Work each side of neck separately.
Dec 1 st at neck edge of next 3 rows, ending with RS
facing for next row, **and at same time** cast off 5 [6: 6:
7: 7] sts at beg of 2nd row.
Cast off rem 5 [5: 6: 6: 8] sts **.
Return to sts left on holder and slip centre 29 [29: 31:
31: 31] sts onto another holder (for neckband). Rejoin
yarn with RS facing and K to end. Complete from * to
** to match first side, reversing shapings.

FRONT
Work as given for back until 4 [4: 6: 6: 6] rows less
have been worked than on back to beg of shoulder
shaping, ending with RS facing for next row.
Shape front neck
Next row (RS): K20 [22: 24: 26: 28] and turn, leaving
rem sts on a holder.
Work each side of neck separately.
Dec 1 st at neck edge of next 3 [3: 4: 4: 4] rows.
17 [19: 20: 22: 24] sts.
Work 0 [0: 1: 1: 1] row, ending with RS facing for next
row.
Shape shoulder
Cast off 5 [6: 6: 7: 7] sts at beg of next and foll alt row
and at same time dec 1 st at neck edge of next and
foll alt row.
Work 1 row.
Cast off rem 5 [5: 6: 6: 8] sts.
Return to sts left on holder and slip centre 25 sts onto
another holder (for neckband). Rejoin yarn with RS
facing and K to end. Complete to match first side,
reversing shapings.

SLEEVES
Using 6mm (US 10) needles and yarn DOUBLE, cast on
27 [29: 29: 29: 31] sts **loosely**.
Work in rib for 6 rows, ending with RS facing for
next row.
Change to 6½mm (US 10.5) needles.
Beg with a K row, now work in st st throughout as folls:
Inc 1 st at each end of 5th [5th: 5th: 3rd: 3rd] and
every foll 6th [6th: 6th: 4th: 4th] row to 35 [37: 51:
33: 41] sts, then on every foll 8th [8th: 8th: 6th: 6th]
row until there are 47 [49: 53: 55: 59] sts.
Cont straight until sleeve meas 48 [48: 49: 49: 49] cm,
ending with RS facing for next row.
Shape top
Cast off 3 sts at beg of next 2 rows. 41 [43: 47: 49: 53] sts.
Dec 1 st at each end of next 3 rows, then on foll alt
row, then on 2 foll 4th rows. 29 [31: 35: 37: 41] sts.
Work 1 row.
Dec 1 st at each end of next and foll 2 [3: 3: 4: 4] alt
rows, then on foll 5 [5: 7: 7: 9] rows, ending with RS
facing for next row.
Cast off rem 13 sts.

MAKING UP
Press as described on the information page.
Join right shoulder seam.
Neckband
With RS facing, using 6mm (US 10) needles and yarn
DOUBLE, pick up and knit 6 [6: 8: 8: 8] sts down left
side of front neck, K across 25 sts on front holder, pick
up and knit 6 [6: 8: 8: 8] sts up right side of front neck,
and 3 sts down right side of back neck, K across
29 [29: 31: 31: 31] sts on back holder inc 1 st at centre,
then pick up and knit 3 sts up left side of back neck.
73 [73: 79: 79: 79] sts.
Beg with row 2, work in rib as given for back for
5 rows, ending with RS facing for next row.
Cast off in rib.
See information page for finishing instructions, setting
in sleeves using the set-in method.

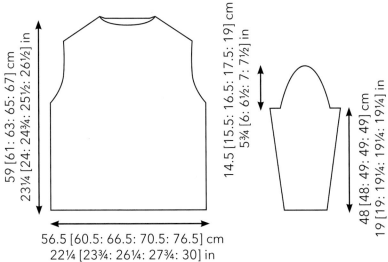

aperol ●●○○

SIZE
133.5 cm / 52½ in long x 50.5 cm / 20 in at widest point

YARN
Rowan Summerlite DK and Kidsilk Haze
SL - Cantaloupe 456
    5   x 50gm
KSH - Golden Poppy 683
    3   x 25gm

NEEDLES
4½mm (no 7) (US 7) needles

TENSION
20 sts and 40 rows to 10 cm / 4 in, measured over pattern using 4½mm needles holding 1 strand of each yarn together throughout

SCARF
Using 4½mm needles and 1 strand of each yarn cast on 101 sts.
Work in g st until work meas 2 cm, ending with a WS row.

Pattern:
Row 1 (RS): Knit
Row 2: Knit
Row 3: K4, K1 * Sl 1 purlwise, K1, rep from * to last 4 sts, K4.
Row 4: K4, K1 * yf, Sl 1 purlwise, yb, K1, rep from * to last 4 sts, K4.
Row 5: Knit
Row 6: Knit
Row 7: K4, K2 * Sl 1 purlwise , K1, rep from * to last 5 sts, K5.
Row 8: K4, K2, * yf, Sl 1 purlwise, yb, K1, rep from * to last 5 sts, K5.
Work in pattern as set above.

Keeping pattern correct, decrease 1 st after first 4 Knit stitches on next and every foll 6th row to 12 sts ending with a WS row.
Next Row (RS): K4, (K2tog) twice, K4. 10 sts
Next Row: Knit
Next Row: K3, (K2tog) twice, K3. 8 sts
Next Row: Knit.
Next Row: K2, (K2tog) twice, K2. 6 sts

Next Row: Knit.
Next Row: K1, (K2tog) twice, K1. 4 sts
Next Row: Knit.
Next Row: (K2tog) twice. 2 sts.
Next Row: K2tog.
Fasten off.

FINISHING
Press as described on the information page.

pina ●●○○

SIZE

To fit bust

81-86	91-97	102-107	112-117	122-127	cm
32-34	36-38	40-42	44-46	48-50	in

Actual bust measurement of garment

92	102.5	113.5	121.5	132	cm
36¼	40¼	44¾	47¾	52	in

YARN

Rowan Cotton Glace

11	12	13	14	15	x 50gm

(photographed in Bleached 726)

NEEDLES

1 pair 3½mm (no 10/9) (US 4) needles
1 pair 4mm (no 8) (US 6) needles
3½mm (no 10/9) (US 4) circular needle at least
100 cm long

TENSION

30 sts and 24 rows to 10 cm / 4 in measured
over patt using 4mm (US 6) needles.

BACK

Using 3½mm (US 4) needles cast on 107 [119: 131:
141: 153] sts.
Row 1 (RS): K1, *P1, K1, rep from * to end.
Row 2: As row 1.
These 2 rows form moss st.
Cont in moss st for a further 7 rows, ending with **WS**
facing for next row.
Row 10 (WS): Moss st 8 [8: 8: 10: 10] sts, M1, (moss st
3 sts, M1) 30 [34: 38: 40: 44] times, moss st 9 [9: 9:
11: 11] sts. 138 [154: 170: 182: 198] sts.
Change to 4mm (US 6) needles.
Cont in patt as folls:
Row 1 (RS): Purl.
Row 2: K1, *(K1, P1, K1) all into next st, P3tog,
rep from * to last st, K1.
Row 3: Purl.
Row 4: K1, *P3tog, (K1, P1, K1) all into next st, rep
from * to last st, K1.
These 4 rows form patt.
Cont straight until back meas 48 [50: 52: 54: 56] cm,
ending with RS facing for next row.
Shape shoulders and back neck
Cast off all sts **knitwise**, placing markers either side
of centre 58 [58: 60: 60: 62] sts (for back neck) – there
will be 40 [48: 55: 61: 68] sts either side (for shoulder
seams).

LEFT FRONT

Using 3½mm (US 4) needles cast on 51 [57: 63:
69: 75] sts.
Work in moss st as given for back for 9 rows, ending
with **WS** facing for next row.
Row 10 (WS): Moss st 4 sts, M1, (moss st 3 sts, M1)
14 [16: 18: 20: 22] times, moss st 5 sts. 66 [74: 82:
90: 98] sts.
Change to 4mm (US 6) needles.
Beg with row 1, work in pattern as given for back until
50 [54: 58: 62: 64] rows less have been worked than
on back to shoulder cast-off, ending with RS facing for
next row.
Shape front slope
Keeping patt correct, dec 1 st at end of next row and
at same edge on foll 6 [2: 0: 0: 0] rows, then on foll
18 [22: 25: 27: 28] alt rows, then on foll 4th row.
40 [48: 55: 61: 68] sts.
Work 3 rows, ending with RS facing for next row.
Shape shoulder
Cast off all sts **knitwise**.

RIGHT FRONT

Using 3½mm (US 4) needles cast on 51 [57: 63:
69: 75] sts.
Work in moss st as given for back for 9 rows, ending
with **WS** facing for next row.
Row 10 (WS): Moss st 4 sts, M1, (moss st 3 sts, M1)
14 [16: 18: 20: 22] times, moss st 5 sts. 66 [74: 82:
90: 98] sts.

Change to 4mm (US 6) needles.
Beg with row 1, now work in patt as given for back and cont straight until 50 [54: 58: 62: 64] rows less have been worked than on back to shoulder cast-off, ending with RS facing for next row.

Shape front slope
Keeping patt correct, dec 1 st at beg of next row and at same edge on foll 6 [2: 0: 0: 0] rows, then on foll 18 [22: 25: 27: 28] alt rows, then on foll 4th row.
40 [48: 55: 61: 68] sts.
Work 3 rows, ending with RS facing for next row.

Shape shoulder
Cast off all sts **knitwise**.

SLEEVES
Using 3½mm (US 4) needles cast on 49 [51: 55: 55: 57] sts.
Work in moss st as given for back for 9 rows, ending with **WS** facing for next row.

Row 10 (WS): Moss st 6 [4: 6: 6: 4] sts, M1, (moss st 3 sts, M1) 12 [14: 14: 14: 16] times, moss st 7 [5: 7: 7: 5] sts. 62 [66: 70: 70: 74] sts.
Change to 4mm (US 6) needles.
Beg with row 1, now work in patt as given for back and cont as folls:
Inc 1 st at each end of 3rd and foll 2 [8: 11: 21: 25] alt rows, then on 20 [17: 16: 11: 9] foll 4th rows, taking inc sts into patt. 108 [118: 126: 136: 144] sts.
Cont straight until sleeve meas 44 [44: 45: 45: 45] cm, ending with RS facing for next row.
Cast off all sts **knitwise**.

MAKING UP
Press as described on the information page.
Join both shoulder seams.

Front band
With RS facing and using 3½mm (US 4) circular needle, beg and ending at front cast-on edges, pick up and knit 62 [62: 67: 67: 67] sts up right front opening edge to beg of front slope shaping, 50 [54: 58: 62: 64] sts up right front slope, 45 [45: 47: 47: 49] sts from back, 50 [54: 58: 62: 64] sts down left front slope to beg of front slope shaping, and 62 [62: 67: 67: 67] sts down left front opening edge. 269 [277: 297: 305: 311] sts.
Work in moss st as given for back for 3 rows, ending with RS facing for next row.

Row 4 (RS): Moss st 4 sts, *yrn, work 2 tog (to make a buttonhole), moss st 9 [9: 10: 10: 10] sts, rep from * 4 times more, yrn, work 2 tog (to make 6th buttonhole), moss st to end.
Work in moss st for a further 5 rows, ending with RS facing for next row.
Cast off in moss st.
Mark points along side seam edges 19 [20.5: 22: 23.5: 25] cm either side of shoulder seams (to denote base of armhole openings). See information page for finishing instructions, setting in sleeves using the straight cast-off method.

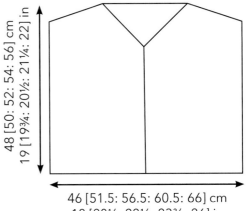

48 [50: 52: 54: 56] cm
19 [19¾: 20½: 21¼: 22] in

46 [51.5: 56.5: 60.5: 66] cm
18 [20¼: 22¼: 23¾: 26] in

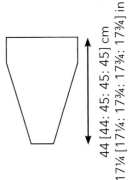

44 [44: 45: 45: 45] cm
17¼ [17¼: 17¼: 17¾: 17¾] in

SIZING

To help you enjoy a great knitting experience and a well fitting garment please refer to our sizing guide which conforms to standard clothing sizes. Dimensions in our sizing guide are body measurements, not garment dimensions, please refer to the size diagram for this measurement.

SIZING GUIDE

UK SIZE	S	M	L	XL	XXL	
To fit bust	32 – 34	36 – 38	40 – 42	44 – 46	48 – 50	inches
	81 – 86	91– 97	102 – 107	112 – 117	122-127	cm
To fit waist	24 – 26	28 – 30	32 – 34	36 – 38	40 – 42	inches
	61 – 66	71 – 76	81 – 86	91 – 97	102 – 107	cm
To fit hips	34 – 36	38 – 40	42 – 44	46 – 48	50 – 52	inches
	86 – 91	97 – 102	107 – 112	117 – 122	127 – 132	cm

SIZING & SIZE DIAGRAM NOTE

The instructions are given for the smallest size. Where they vary, work the figures in brackets for the larger sizes. One set of figures refers to all sizes. Included with most patterns in this magazine is a 'size diagram' - see image on the right, of the finished garment and its dimensions. The measurement shown at the bottom of each 'size diagram' shows the garment width 2.5cm below the armhole shaping. To help you choose the size of garment to knit please refer to the sizing guide. Generally in the majority of designs the welt width (at the cast on edge of the garment) is the same width as the chest. However, some designs may be 'A-Line' in shape or flared edge and in these cases welt width will be wider than the chest width.

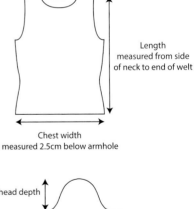

Length
measured from side
of neck to end of welt

Chest width
measured 2.5cm below armhole

Sleeve head depth

Underarm
measured from end
of cuffs to armhole

MEASURING GUIDE

For maximum comfort and to ensure the correct fit when choosing a size to knit, please follow the tips below when checking your size. Measure yourself close to your body, over your underwear and don't pull the tape measure too tight!

Bust/chest - measure around the fullest part of the bust/chest and across the shoulder blades.

Waist - measure around the natural waistline, just above the hip bone.

Hips - measure around the fullest part of the bottom.

If you don't wish to measure yourself, note the size of a favourite jumper that you like the fit of. Our sizes are now comparable to the clothing sizes from the major high street retailers, so if your favourite jumper is a size Medium or size 12, then our Medium should be approximately the same fit. To be extra sure, measure your favourite jumper and then compare these measurements with the Rowan size diagram given at the end of the individual instructions.

Finally, once you have decided which size is best for you, please ensure that you achieve the tension required for the design you wish to knit.

Remember if your tension is too loose, your garment will be bigger than the pattern size and you may use more yarn. If your tension is too tight, your garment could be smaller than the pattern size and you will have yarn left over.

Furthermore if your tension is incorrect, the handle of your fabric will be too stiff or floppy and will not fit properly. It really does make sense to check your tension before starting every project.

PHOTOGRAPHY MODEL SIZING

The model used in this collection wears a UK dress size 8. Wearing garments that were knitted in a bust size 32 - 34". Height: 173cm / 5ft 8in

ABBREVIATIONS

alt	alternate
beg	begin(ning)
cm	centimetres
cont	continue
C4F	slip next 2 stitches onto a cable needle and hold in front of work, knit next 2 stitches, knit 2 stitches from cable needle.
C3F	slip next 2 sts onto cable needle and leave at front of work, K1, then K2 from cable needle.
dec	decrease(s)(ing)
foll(s)	follow(s)(ing)
g	grams
g st	garter stitch (knit all rows)
in	inch(es)
inc	increase(s)(ing)
K	knit
Kfb	knit in front and back of stitch (makes 1stitch)
M1	make 1 stitch
meas	measures
mm	millimetres
P	purl
patt	pattern
psso	pass slipped stitch over
rem	remain(ing)
rep	repeat
RS	right side of work
Sl 1	slip 1 stitch
st st	stocking stitch (knit on RS rows, purl on WS rows)
st(s)	stitch(es)
tbl	through back of loop
tog	together
WS	wrong side of work

TENSION

This is the size of your knitting. Most of the knitting patterns will have a tension quoted. This is how many stitches 10cm/4in in width and how many rows 10cm/4in in length to make a square. If your knitting doesn't match this then your finished garment will not measure the correct size. To obtain the correct measurements for your garment you must achieve the tension.

The tension quoted on a ball band is the manufacturer's average. For the manufacturer and designers to produce designs they have to use a tension for you to be able to obtain the measurements quoted. It's fine not to be the average, but you need to know if you meet the average or not. Then you can make the necessary adjustments to obtain the correct measurements.

CHOOSING YARN

All the colours and textures, where do you start? Look for the thickness, how chunky do you want your finished garment? Sometimes it's colour that draws you to a yarn or perhaps you have a pattern that requires a specific yarn. Check the washing/care instructions before you buy.

Yarn varies in thickness; there are various descriptions such as DK and 4ply these are examples of standard weights. There are a lot of yarns available that are not standard and it helps to read the ball band to see what the recommended needle size is.

This will give you an idea of the approximate thickness. It is best to use the yarn recommended in the pattern. Keep one ball band from each project so that you have a record of what you have used and most importantly how to care for your garment after it has been completed. Always remember to give the ball band with the garment if it is a gift.

The ball band normally provides you with the average tension and recommended needle sizes for the yarn, this may vary from what has been used in the pattern, always go with the pattern as the designer may change needles to obtain a certain look. The ball band also tells you the name of the yarn and what it is made of, the weight and approximate length of the ball of yarn along with the shade and dye lot numbers. This is important as dye lots can vary, you need to buy your yarn with matching dye lots.

PRESSING AND AFTERCARE

Having spent so long knitting your project it can be a great shame not to look after it properly. Some yarns are suitable for pressing once you have finished to improve the look of the fabric. To find out this information you will need to look on the yarn ball band, where there will be washing and care symbols.

Once you have checked to see if your yarn is suitable to be pressed and the knitting is a smooth texture (stocking stitch for example), pin out and place a damp cloth onto the knitted pieces. Hold the steam iron (at the correct temperature) approximately 10cm/4in away from the fabric and steam. Keep the knitted pieces pinned in place until cool.

As a test it is a good idea to wash your tension square in the way you would expect to wash your garment.

EXPERIENCE RATING
for guidance only

● **BEGINNER TECHNIQUES**

For the beginner knitter, basic garment shaping and straight forward stitch technique.

●● **SIMPLE TECHNIQUES**

Simple straight forward knitting, introducing various, shaping techniques and garments.

●●● **EXPERIENCE TECHNIQUES**

For the more experienced knitter, using more advanced shaping techniques at the same time as colourwork or more advanced stitch techniques.

●●●● **ADVANCED TECHNIQUES**

Advanced techniques used, using advanced stitches and garment shaping along with more challenging techniques.